# Abused, Victimized, & Traumatized

# ABUSED, VICTIMIZED, & TRAUMATIZED

## An Idiot's Guide to Management

*Dazed, Crazed, and Confused*

Writers Club Press
San Jose New York Lincoln Shanghai

**Abused, Victimized, & Traumatized**
**An Idiot's Guide to Management**



Writers Club Press
an imprint of iUniverse, Inc.

For information address:
iUniverse, Inc.
5220 S. 16th St., Suite 200
Lincoln, NE 68512
www.iuniverse.com

ISBN: 0-595-21283-2

Printed in the United States of America

*The current book is intended as a humorous and satirical work of fiction.*

*The characters and events in this book are fictitious. Any similarity to real persons, living or dead, is coincidental and not intended by the authors.*

*As the current book is fictional and aimed at humor, the authors assume no responsibility for any actions that a reader may take, based upon the writings or thoughts contained herein.*

*For every employee who has worked for an idiot.*

# *Contents*

# A Pointer Before

What keeps civilization civilized? Managers. Managers preserve the civility of modern civilization by maintaining a strict control over the barbaric hoards of employees. Often this is not an easy task and subsequently there is the need for assisting managers in realizing their full potential.

The current work is predicated on the belief that abused, victimized, and traumatized employees are often the result of management by an idiot. In recognition that the majority of employees will claim that they have been abused, victimized, and traumatized, the current work is aimed at providing specific guidelines and examples that will enable a person to become an idiot and subsequently engage in successful management.

The current book is primarily divided into the following three (3) major sections:

Classical Examples
Declaration of War
Tactical Advice

The "***Classical Examples***" section provides examples from history where managers demonstrated the ability to overcome the barbaric hoards of employees.

The "***Declaration of War***" details the elemental attributes necessary in beginning the journey of becoming a successful manager. Without recognizing basic tenants, as true, a potential manager will never be capable of exercising the elements provided in the "***Tactical Advice***" section.

The "***Tactical Advice***" section not only provides examples of effective management, but also provides practical managerial tools.

After presenting the above information, the current book finally provides a sample "***Self Assessment***" section which is designed to evaluate your effectiveness as a manager.

Know that others have gone before you and have not only survived, but achieved greatness.

# *Definition of Terms*

## Abused:

Webster's Dictionary defines "***abuse***" as "***use wrongly***" and "***mistreatment.***" While employees are typically hired to perform specific duties, managers often "***use wrongly***" employees through requiring the employees to perform duties outside of their job description. These "duties" are often utilized by managers, in order to highlight the distinction between employer and employee, with these "duties" often including such activities as washing the manager's car, dropping off personal mail for the manager, and any other activity that the manager deems important. While the manager may not specifically state that if the employee doesn't perform these duties that their job will be terminated, there is the implication that completing these other duties may aid in gaining the manager's favor. An "***abused***" employee becomes an employee that has lost all recollection as to what their actual job duties entail and relies solely on the manager to enlighten them regarding their duties. The "***abused***" employee arrives to work every day and receives daily instruction from their manager as to what duties are to be accomplished.

## Victimized:

Webster's Dictionary defines "**victim**" as "***one killed, hurt, etc.; one cheated, tricked, etc.***" and "***victimize***" as "***make a victim of.***" (Webster's New World Compact, Dictionary of American English, Simon

& Schuster, New York, 1981). Employees typically are at the workplace for eight (8) hours a day, five (5) days a week. Consider that when employees leave the workplace and think about their managers during their off hours (away from the workplace), they're not getting paid. When employees awaken in the morning and their first thought is about their supervisor and whether they will come to work, they aren't getting compensated. In essence, the managerial style that causes employees to think about work, when they're not at work, cheats the employee of their personal time; their time away from work.

## Traumatized:

Webster's Dictionary defines "***trauma***" as "***bodily injury; emotional shock with lasting psychic effects.***" (Webster's New World Compact, Dictionary of American English, Simon & Schuster, New York, 1981). The managerial style that causes emotional shock to an employee is not something that is easily treated by the medical profession.

Without going to the extreme of electrical shock therapy, there is little that can be done to prevent memories from surfacing in one's mind. Subsequently, the utilization of a specific managerial style cannot only have the effect of causing an employee to become a victim, but it can also ensure that the employee will be forever embroiled in painful memories.

## Idiot:

Webster's Dictionary defines "***Idiot***" as "***Person who is mentally very deficient.***" As applied to managerial style, mental deficiency may be neither a pre-existing condition nor permanent. Specifically, an "***idiot***" manager may have a normal life outside of the work environment (***Writer's Note: Though this is a rare occurrence, as an idiot manager tends to continue the role of an idiot into all phases***

***of his life***), and, with the right conditioning, an intelligent person can be reduced to a blubbering idiot upon their rise to a managerial position. In addition, the mental deficiency is often self-induced, as a means to rationalize irrational behavior. An example. A manager does something that is highly irrational (stupid often being used in place of the term irrational) and then rationalizes that the behavior was the result of inexperience (not the manager's inexperience, but the employee's).

# *Classical Examples*

Throughout recorded history, there have been numerous examples of effective leadership through the application of victimizing and traumatizing employees.

## The Great Wall of China:

It is estimated that in the 3rd Century (BC), construction of a wall was initiated, in order to protect China from intruders. The construction of the "***Great Wall of China***" stands as a monument to the accomplishments that can be achieved through effective leadership. While it's only a rumor that occasionally the employees constructing the wall would end up inside the wall, it wouldn't be a totally bad managerial option. You have a problem employee that just won't become a team player and you need to get this huge wall built. Solution. You make the employee a part of the solution by adding him to the wall. As an interesting side note, the Great Wall of China is not a continuous structure, rather it is a system of walls and towers, with gaps in certain places which enabled intruders to entry.

***Lesson Learned:*** If an employee won't willingly contribute to the project, make them a part of the project.

## Pyramids:

The pyramids of Egypt are a spectacular sight. Did you know that pyramids weren't constructed for utilization as office buildings, but were constructed primarily for the purpose of burying supervisors? Historians now agree that the pyramids were neither built by slaves nor war captives, but by regular Egyptians. What a magnificent example of effective leadership to have your employees build a monument to you.

***Lesson Learned*:** Never let employees know the true purpose of their efforts.

## General George Washington:

On December 26, 1776, General George Washington, commander of the American revolutionary force, led troops across the Delaware River, in a surprise attack on the English and Hessian troops . A painter caught the intensity of the moment by showing General Washington, standing up in the boat, while his troops rowed the boat across the river. General Washington showed the genius of managing by discarding safe boating practices and rising above his troops.

***Lesson Learned*:** Even if an action goes against common sense, always be above your troops.

## The French Revolution:

During the French Revolution, many an aristocrat was led to the guillotine. Now, some may argue that this was a movement against aristocratic management, but this is untrue. The aristocrats were merely projected images of the real managers. By allowing the masses to believe that they were ridding France of aristocratic rule, the true managers (behind the scenes) were removing the competition.

***Lesson Learned:*** When it becomes necessary to sabotage another manager, make it appear that it was what the masses wanted and you were powerless to stop them.

## Nero:

There is the often told story of how, when Rome was burning to the ground, that Emperor Nero bounded up to the roof of the palace, threw on the harpist's garb, and let loose with a chorus of song. While the people of Rome were thrown into a panic, and countless lives were being lost, Emperor Nero displayed the characteristics of a true supervisor, by ignoring practical sense (getting some water and helping to put out the fire), and engaging in behavior that seems odd.

***Lesson Learned:*** Even when your empire is burning, never let your employees see fear in your eyes because, like dogs, employees can smell fear.

## Marie Antoinette:

During the French Revolution, Marie Antoinette demonstrated the sensitivity of an effective manager. When advised that the lower classes of France were starving and their supply of bread was running extremely low, Ms. Antoinette reportedly issued the directive, "***Let them eat cake.***"

***Lesson Learned:*** A good boss will occasionally let their employees enjoy a celebration.

## General George Custer:

In 1876, the 7th United States Cavalry Regiment, under Lieutenant Colonel George Armstrong Custer, was assigned to complete a task of finding some Indians. During a managerial meeting, Lieutenant Colonel Custer declined the offer of the Gatling gun battery (a formidable weapon), by stating that this added piece of equipment would hinder his progress in accomplishing the goals of his superiors. Lieutenant Colonel Custer further declined to accept the assistance of four (4) companies of cavalry, by stating that the 7$^{th}$ Cavalry could handle the task at hand, without any assistance. After the managerial meeting, Lieutenant Colonel Custer led his employees to a location known as the Rosebud-Little Big Horn divide, where they met a large group of unhappy customers which left Lieutenant Colonel Custer and his employees in a dead state.

***Lessons Learned:*** First, when your upper management offers either equipment or personnel, always refuse, as this shows that you can achieve the goal without any help. Secondly, if you present a lie as truth (i.e., There are no Indians and everything will be all right) and with a certain degree of enthusiasm, then your employees will come to believe the lie to be true.

## Robin Hood:

In England, a supervisor, by the name of Robin Hood, gained a certain degree of notoriety as being a leader of "***Merry Men.***" Robin Hood and his merry men steal from the rich and give to the poor. They fight the injustices of the world and save fair maidens from evil lords (upper managers). Robin Hood stands as a truly great supervisor for the following reasons:

1. He convinced his employees that they were stealing from the rich and giving to the poor, with this bringing a sense of noble pur-

pose for his employees, when in actuality Robin Hood was supplementing his 401-K.

2. He convinced a group of grown men that wearing green tights was stylish.

3. He convinced his employees that sleeping on the cold, hard ground was fun.

***Lesson Learned:*** Develop a noble cause with which your employees can identify. A secondary lesson would be to create the illusion of unity by having all of your employees dress the same. This is an important lesson, as in the event of a rebellion, your employees will be easily spotted.

# *Declaration of War*

How many victories have been declared which were not first preceded by a war? It is a basic tenant that in order to achieve victory, then there must first be a battle.

If you intend to have victory over employees, then you must first realize that war is constantly being waged between employees and managers. While employees may be mislead into believing that their employment is a career, you, as a manager, must never view the relationship between employees and management as either cordial or professional; it's war.

Assuming the belief that employment is war, then how does one win the war and achieve victory?

## War:

The "***Art of War***" has been recognized as a classical study of strategy, as applied to war. Sun Tzu also showed an insight into managerial strategy by advising:

> ***"Know the enemy and know yourself, and in a hundred battles you will never be defeated. If you know only yourself, not the enemy, your chances of winning and losing are equal. If you are ignorant of either the enemy or yourself, you will surely be defeated in every battle."***

## Know the Enemy:

Before you arrive at a new office, it is important to know the employees who you will be supervising. This can be accomplished by contacting managers who have previously supervised the employees. This will aid in identifying those employees who will most likely be a problem or attempt to usurp your authority. However, be careful of the manager that touts any employee as being an outstanding employee, as it is most likely a desire of that manager to never supervise the employee again because the employee is NOT outstanding. It is a common practice of some managers to give glowing recommendations of employees that they would like to see disappear.

Once you arrive at an office, it is often helpful to play the part of a friend, in order to learn the attributes of your employees (enemies). Encourage them to discuss their personal lives and any problems they may be experiencing. In later encounters, this will help you to know where the employee's weaknesses lie and allow you to devise appropriate strategies.

As a manager, you should be aware that every employee, in some fashion, is the enemy. Employees either want to join the ranks of management or they want to overthrow management.

## Know Yourself:

As Sun Tzu suggested, it is important to know the enemy, as well as yourself. Before you begin a new supervisory assignment, it is important to take account of yourself. Ask yourself the following questions:

1. ***What are my physical attributes?***

2. ***What is the extent of my intellect?***

3. ***How much experience do I possess in my job?***

4. ***What are my accomplishments, in my job?***

5. ***What is the extent of my ability to communicate?***

Now, dismiss your answers. You can be tall or short, you can be obese or thin, you can be ugly or you can be attractive. You can be intelligent or unintelligent. You can possess volumes of experience or you can possess no experience. You can point to significant accomplishments or you can lack a single accomplishment. You can communicate with the ease of a politician or you can stammer. You can write with the flair of a poet or you can write as a slow kindergarten student.

None of this matters. The only thing that matters is that you are a supervisor, you are a member of the elite. You don't have to prove anything to anyone, and especially to subordinates.

Again, the only thing to know about yourself is that you are a manager.

# *Tactical Advice*

In this section, you will be provided with either examples or scenarios aimed at improving your management of subordinates.

## Divide and Conquer

Few supervisors are born into a managerial position and alongside subordinates. Subsequently, the majority of supervisors will experience those occasions when they assume a new position which will involve assuming the managerial reins over new people. In recognition of this eventuality, the following provides a method of cementing new relationships.

The first time you actually meet your subordinates, it is very important to stress that you're on a higher level. This can be accomplished a number of ways, but the most effective means is through conducting an office meeting with all subordinates.

You must demonstrate from the very beginning that you are fashion-conscious and are willing to spare no expense in dressing the part of a manager. If your subordinates are inclined to wearing casual attire, then you must, I repeat, you must wear a tie and coat. You must also wear a white shirt, as it is universally accepted as a symbol of purity.

Situate yourself at the head of the table. If you're height-challenged, it may be necessary to bring some telephone books prior to the meeting and place them on your chair. It is important that you not only represent yourself as being superior intellectually, but also that you assume the high ground.

If you allow yourself to become of "***one of the guys***", you will have lost all division between management and subordinates. Consequently, it becomes necessary to draw a distinction between yourself (a manager) and your subordinates (peons). This can be accomplished, not only by the tilt of your nose in an upward position, but also through verbal statements. As subordinates tend to be focused on personal comfort, rather than on moving up the corporate ladder, you can create an effective division by identifying those activities that you (as a manager—someone significantly higher than subordinates) do not engage. The following is intended as examples and can be modified for each situation:

***"I don't smoke."***

***"I don't drink."***

***"I don't go to parties."***

***"I don't associate with subordinates."***

***"I've been married to the same person for over 25 years."***

Make it clear from the start that you're the manager and that subordinates are inferior, not only in the workplace, but also on a social setting. Make it clear that even if you inadvertently meet in a social setting, that you would not be inclined to associate with your subordinates.

If you made the mistake of majoring in a scientific or job-specific course of college study (such as Criminal Justice, Biology, Engineering, etc.), it is imperative that you don't let your subordinates learn of this mistake. To be a successful manager, you must have majored in a field of study that has no correlation to a job. Consider, if you are superior, then why would you need to study subjects relating to a job? Perhaps, the best major to either complete or tell your employees that you completed, is English. English is effective for the following reasons:

1. When you correct your employees' work products, you can cite your knowledge of English and proper grammar. This makes you not only appear to have more knowledge, but also removes the potential for any disagreements.

2. When an employee makes a written suggestion, you can tell them that you need to review the product. When you review the product, you can make changes that will make you look better and your employee look stupid. You can make these changes on the basis that **YOUR** wording, based on sound English techniques, makes more sense to the reader. In essence, you can change reports to suit your own agenda. In addition, you can keep changing reports until the report becomes what was originally submitted.

3. When an employee engages in a verbal confrontation where you don't have a clue regarding what they're talking about, you can lean your head back, place your fingertips together, and let out a sigh. The employee then thinks that you're considering what they've said, when in actuality you're trying to think of what to say. You can also use this break to think about who you can call, in order to get an answer. After you've had some time to think and consult with other authorities, you can then get back to the employee and present the perfect response (at least in your mind).

***Lessons Learned:*** When you first meet your subordinates, it is important to effectively establish a division between them (inferior) and you (superior).

## Snitches

First, what is a snitch?

Quite simply, a "***snitch***" is an employee, who desires to be in management, but will never rise to such a level. However, the employee doesn't like his fellow employees and considers himself to be above his fellow employees. Being unable to become a manager and feeling above his fellow employees, a snitch becomes an employee, who vents their frustration with their dismal situation through informing on the misbehavior (actual or created) of his coworkers to management. When the old adage, "***The walls have ears***", is referenced, it is in direct reference to snitches.

The utilization of snitches is often an underestimated tool of effective management. Snitches or sources of information are effective in several ways. First, as a manager, it is important to know any indicators of a possible attempt to either undermine or usurp your power. A snitch can provide you with what the troops are doing and what the troops are planning and what the troops are saying about you. Utilizing a snitch allows you to avoid the expense of using listening devices in your employees' offices or lunchroom. Some employees, after watching those ridiculous television shows, have learned about the placement of microphones and miniature cameras. However, a snitch, a really good one, can make the pretense of being one of the group and subsequently can gain first-hand knowledge of what the troops are doing.

A snitch is also effective in another way. If you are successful in preempting a revolution, then you can casually state that you gained the information from a snitch. Workers will focus their anger on identifying the snitch, rather than being upset with you for using a snitch. And, with the employees trying to identify the snitch, they aren't as busy with trying to usurp your power.

A snitch is also effective in showing other employees that service to you results in rewards. It doesn't matter if your snitch is incompetent. However, it is important that you reward your snitch through employee appraisals and awards. At office meetings wherein you reward or acknowledge the accomplishments (real or imaginary) of your snitch, you highlight that employees are rewarded not for doing their job, but for doing your bidding.

A snitch is also invaluable in making strategic attacks against other employees. When you want to berate an employee, you conveniently conduct the session with only that employee and the snitch. The snitch then serves as a witness to whatever you want to say took place in the session. Depending on the situation, the snitch can exaggerate the actions of the other employee.

An example. You call an employee into the office (with the snitch present). You tell the employee that he's incompetent, inexperienced, and lucky to have a job. The employee asks what he can do to improve (like that's possible). You tell the employee that the meeting is over (this reinforces to the employee that they are indeed incompetent and can't improve). This event, with the assistance of the snitch, can then be memorialized, in writing, as occurring like this: As an understanding and compassionate supervisor, you conducted a meeting with an employee wherein you encouraged the employee to take specific steps to improve their work products. The employee became hostile (through the nature of his question) and stormed out of your office. With your snitch as a witness, the truth of the event becomes two (you and your snitch) to one. Besides, you're a supervisor and they don't make liars supervisors and your snitch (through your efforts) has a demonstrated history of receiving recognition and awards. In addition, since a snitch can't think for themselves, they can testify to whatever you tell them.

It is also important to maintain a derogatory file on your snitches. In the event that your snitch lose his loyalty to you, then you will have something to blackmail the snitch with, in order to keep both his loyalty and silence.

Even when you leave a position, **ALWAYS** retain your snitches. This way you can continue to be apprised of what's going on, as well as to continue to mettle in the affairs of your former employees.

***Lesson Learned:*** A snitch in the time of trouble is worth their weight in gold.

## The Hunt

Because employees are extremely nervous about you knowing what they are doing, they are extremely paranoid. This paranoia is largely based on the employees' knowledge that they are inferior. A scared employee is a productive employee. In order to increase the level of fear, it is often helpful to shadow an employee. When the employee leaves the office, you merely follow them. When they go into the Post Office, you go into the Post Office. If the employee questions you, you just ignore their question and intensify their fear by stating that this is the Post Office you always frequent (especially when you know that they know that you live over 20 miles in the other direction, with another Post Office being across the street from your house).

You will only have to follow an employee until they know that you are following them. When they know that you are following them, then they will suspect that you're always following them. This increases their paranoia and makes them more attentive to working.

***Lesson Learned:*** European aristocracy had their foxhunts. It is your right, as a manager, to have your "***employee hunt***."

## The Look

There are two (2) old adages: "***If looks could kill, you'd be dead***"; and "***A picture is worth a thousand words.***" If appropriately applied, these two (2) adages can help you to subdue your subordinates.

Developing a "***look that can kill***" takes a great deal of practice. This isn't something that is easily accomplished. You don't want to have a look that makes your employees laugh, rather than cringe. It's recommended that you practice your "***look***" by staring into a mirror and creating a "***look***" that is compatible with your facial contour. Some supervisors utilize the "***look***" by furrowing their brows. Some supervisors utilize the "***look***" by clenching their jaws together and smiling with clenched teeth. Other supervisors utilize the "***look***" by scrunching their nose and take deep breaths, with this breathing technique resulting in their nostrils flaring (much like a horse). After you've developed your own unique "***look***", it's further recommended that you test your "***look***" on small children. If they run away crying, then you've developed a successful "***look***", because employees are much like small children.

In reference to "***A picture is worth a thousand words***", you can use your developed look and expound on it. An example, when an employee asks a stupid question, you give them a modified look which (without any words leaving your mouth), that they're stupid, you wonder how they can be so stupid, get out of my sight, how could you (the employee) have lived so long, and many other words that summarize your disgust with the employee. Developing the "***look***" and using it, rather than verbalization, takes a great deal of practice. However, after you've developed the "***look***", you will find that it is almost an automatic function. An employee does something stupid, **BAM**, you give them the "***look***."

***Lesson Learned:*** If you've got the "***look***", then small children and employees alike will flee from your presence.

## Helping Hand

The majority of employees mistakenly believe that they possess attributes which will allow them to "***move up the ladder.***" This is a mistaken belief because employees are all inferior and possess no redeeming qualities. If employees were allowed to "***move up the ladder***", then there would be utter chaos and your position as a manager would be threatened. When your position is threatened, then the whole hierarchy of management becomes threatened. Consequently, it is your duty, no it is your obligation, to prevent employees from "***moving up the ladder.***"

When an employee applies for a transfer or promotion, it is necessary for you to offer your honest opinion to the hiring/promoting official. It is important to display the employee as a "***trouble-maker***", a malcontent, a slacker, incompetent, inexperienced, and, in general terms, unqualified to even hold their current position. It doesn't matter whether this is true or not, because once you express your opinions, the hiring/promoting official will begin to think about what you've said. However, your input predisposes them to thinking of the employee in negative terms. This is especially helpful in those occasions where an employee actually has a great deal of experience and has received numerous awards for their job performance.

You can add further doubt on the employee's capability by anticipating a review of the employee's work history and job performance. You diminish the employee's work experience by dropping the comment, "***I heard that the employee's prior managers gave the employee false accolades because they were friends.***" You can further "help" the employee by stating your opinion, "***I personally believe that sometimes managers give glowing reviews of those employees that they would like to remove.***"

***Lesson Learned:*** It reflects negatively on you, as a manager, when an employee tries to leave. It is a sign that you can't control your employees.

## Door Privileges

If employees experience any type of freedom in the workplace, then they will attempt to extend that freedom to other areas, to include overthrowing your authority. Subsequently, it is necessary to restrict their freedom, at every possible occasion.

An example. In offices where there is a back door, employees will often use this back door for their convenience This convenience is often perceived by employees as a sort of freedom. They can come and go, as they feel. You can vividly demonstrate the extent of your authority by restricting an employee's use of the back door. You tell the employee that they must use the front door. Not only do you disrupt the employee's convenience, but you instill the belief that they have no freedom of movement in and out of the office.

It should be noted that door privileges are directly related to your point of view (no, not your opinion). If your office provides an unhindered view of the front door, then by restricting an employee to using the front door, you can more closely monitor their activities (i.e., when they arrive and when they leave). If your office provides an unhindered view of the back door, then you would naturally restrict the employee to the back door.

***Lesson Learned:*** By back door or front door, know where your employee is going.

## Heartbreaker

There has been much talk about job-related stress. For the record, there is no medical device that can attribute an employee's high blood pressure directly back to you. In essence, you can cause an employee's blood pressure to rise, you can cause an employee to lose sleep, you can cause an employee to develop ulcers, but none of these ailments can be positively attributed to you. In the event that you're ever questioned regarding an employee's statement that you've caused them on-the-job-stress, here are some possible statements that you can make:

1. You've tried to help the employee improve their job performance, but you've noticed that they're really not concerned

about improving. Perhaps, their stress is coming from their inability to perform their job.

2. You've noticed that the employee has made statements about personal problems at home. Perhaps, their stress is caused from their inability to handle personal problems. You know that they've shown that they can't handle problems on the job (***NOTE: Always use any opportunity to highlight that a complaining employee is also a poor employee***).

3. While you're not specifically trained, you have noticed that the employee comes in on Monday mornings with bloodshot eyes. You've also noticed that the employee often returns from a late lunch smelling like alcohol. Perhaps, the employee has problems with alcohol and, heaven forbid, drugs. Of course, the employee's poor job performance could be attributed to their being under the influence of alcohol and/or drugs (***NOTE: Always use any opportunity to highlight that a complaining employee is also a poor employee***).

4. You've been a supervisor for a number of years and you've come to realize that some employees just don't like to be supervised; they're constant complainers. Perhaps, the employee is upset because they don't like to be supervised and will **NEVER** have a good supervisor (***NOTE: Highlight that the problem is with the employee, not you***).

5. While you're no medical doctor, you find it difficult to believe that you could press a specific button and cause another person to experience physical ailments. If this was true, then you would be pressing buttons to cause your mother-in-law ulcers (***NOTE: Sometimes a little humor will show the level of absurdity of the allegation***).

6. Take the offensive. While you find it difficult to believe that you have caused any stress on an employee, you do know that the employee has caused you a great deal of concern, due to their inability to perform their duties (***NOTE: Always use any opportunity to highlight that a complaining employee is also a poor employee***).

***Lesson Learned:*** You know that you've been a successful manager, when an employee's ailments disappear, when you leave.

## It Isn't Discrimination If You Treat Them All the Same

Okay, it is impossible to have all the same type of employee under your supervision. You'll probably have to supervise both females and males. How can you discriminate and keep it from looking like discrimination? This is an easy matter to solve; you simply treat all your employees in the same bad fashion. If anyone raises the complaint of discrimination, you'll be able to emphatically state that you treat all the employees the same (even though the treatment is bad).

***Lesson Learned:*** Treat all employees the same (preferably in a bad fashion).

## You Say Retaliation, I Say Employee Improvement

Invariably, you'll have at least one employee that will file a complaint against you or will just "***rub***" you the wrong way. You've achieved the position of a supervisor, and it's only fair that you get to use your position to retaliate against those who have affronted you. While retaliation is an accepted practice, you must be careful in the manner in which you engage in retaliatory actions. While your primary thought is retaliation, you must couch your reprisal on some justifiable reason.

An example. You want to send an employee on a temporary duty assignment, in order to get them out of the office and out of your sight (***NOTE: This is especially nice, when the assignment occurs at an inconvenient time for the employee and you know the employee won't want to travel***). You also know that sending the employee on the assignment will cause them a great deal of personal discomfort (i.e., they'll be away from home for over 30 days, they'll have to get someone to watch their house, pick up their mail, they had prior personal plans (vacation), etc.). However, you can't just send the employee on the assignment and state that this action is retaliation. You have to be more subtle. You write down this rationale and place in the safe place for future use:

"Employee is being sent on an assignment because it will broaden their professional experience."

In essence, you're sending the employee on the assignment, in order to help their career (if any complaints are filed), but in actuality, you're sending them on assignment as retaliation.

***Lesson Learned:*** It's not what you do that counts, rather it's how you rationalize it.

## Ample Opportunity for Equality

Some managers believe that they should be careful, as their actions might result in an Equal Employment Opportunity (EEO) complaint being brought against them. This shouldn't be a concern for the following reasons:

1. Any legal action is leveled against either the company or the agency,Not you.

2. EEO complaints usually take years to resolve, during which time you are free to continue taking actions against the employee, with impunity.

3. If you treat all employees as inferior, there's no discrimination.

4. EEO is merely an extension of management and gives employees the false sense that their concerns are being acted upon. EEO isn't there to help employees.

5. You're always provided the opportunity to respond to the EEO complaint. This is when pre-prepared memoranda detailing the employee's deficiencies are aptly used. This also provides you an opportunity to further berate the employee to another department. ***Tactical Advice: Put the blame on the employee.***

6. In the event that an EEO complaint is decided against you, then upper management will often provide you one of two options: (1) A transfer to a desirable location; or (2) A promotion. Depending on your aspirations, an EEO complaint can be a very positive thing and that's the truth.

As in the chapter, "***It Isn't Discrimination If You Treat Them All the Same***", you can effectively avoid the appearance of EEO complaints, by treating all of your employees in the same bad manner.

***Lesson Learned:*** Give all employees the equal opportunity to misbehave.

## Achilles Heel Vs Manager's Fist

In Greek mythology, the strongest and most fearless warrior was named Achilles. Legend records that Achilles' mother dipped him into a river which made him invulnerable everywhere. Unfortunately for Achilles, his mother forgot about the part from which she dangled him into the river; his heel. Achilles was eventually killed by being wounded, you guessed it, in the heel.

In a similar fashion, when managers become managers, they are dipped into a pool (the substance is a secret, but usually emits a foul smell) to provide them with the same level of protection. However, unlike Achilles, there is no weak spot in a manager, as a manager rules through their fist. Basically, if you keep the employees under your fist, they can't find a weakness.

In the prior "***Divide & Conquer***" chapter, it was suggested that you make statements, to include, "***I don't drink***", "***I don't smoke***", "***I don't go to parties***", ***and "I've been married to the same person for over 25 years.***" At the time that you make these statements, if you're not drinking, not smoking, not at a party, and still married (or haven't been caught cheating on your spouse), these statements are all true. It is important not to let your employees know that you occasionally smoke, you like to drink (even to the point of being an alcoholic), you attend the "***right***" parties (with your upper management doing the same thing), and you may be inclined to fool around behind your spouse's back.

***Lesson Learned:*** In the eyes of your employees, you must be perfect. What you do when they're not watching (or can't be proved) isn't important.

## Frivolity

You must realize that work is not designed to be an enjoyable activity and consequently, whenever an employee is happy, it must mean that they are conspiring to usurp your authority. The employee is happy because they anticipate that their evil plans will come to fruition. Another reason that employees will laugh and/or be happy is when they're making jokes about you, their supervisor. Whatever the reason(s), when an employee is happy at work, they will become less susceptible to being controlled by you. When the employee is happy, they feel that they have no concerns, no cares, and certainly no boss. It is for these reasons that you must not allow any type of frivolity in the office.

You can achieve this goal by emphasizing that the office is a place where serious work is being conducted and that frivolity gives the impression that the employees aren't taking their jobs seriously. To keep employees immersed in this belief, you can also strategically place posters throughout the office proclaiming, "***No Frivolity In This Office.***"

***Lesson Learned:*** A happy employee is a conspiring employee.

## A Rolling Stone Gathers No Lawsuits

Often, managers will become complacent in their position and begin to enjoy their particular office. Things are going good, the employees are harassed, but haven't filed too many complaints, upper management is pleased with your progress because of your skill in embellishing the facts of tricky situations, and generally, you're happy. This is bad. When you are the most comfortable, this is when really bad things will happen. After you've been in an office for a certain period of time (usually between 2 and 3 years), your employees will begin to learn your behaviorism and patterns. When they feel that they know how you will react, they will then start to plan schemes to overthrow you. This is why, it is important to never stay in one office beyond an acceptable time.

Also, moving from office to office gives the appearance that you're moving up and gaining more and more experience and makes you believe that you're not running from fear, as the employees are usually planning a hostile takeover.

***Lesson Learned:*** Before you're served with lawsuit papers, either move to another office or obtain a promotion.

## Singing Your Own Tune

Despite your attempts and cultivation of snitches, invariably, an allegation will escape from your control and will be referred to either upper management or law enforcement. In the event that this happens, remember everything that you've learned so far. Never make statements in front of witnesses. Only make statements in front of trusted snitches.

As a side-note, you should be aware that snitches, by their mere definition, are not the most trustworthy of individuals. Knowing this slight character flaw, you should realize that, in the event a snitch is pulled in for questioning, they may decide to give you up. For this reason, it's important to either have multiple snitches or some really good photographs of your upper managers engaged in questionable activities.

***Lesson Learned:*** Snitches and photographs are the best preventive medicine to attempted mutinies.

## It's Going In Your Permanent Record

Here's a little secret that will enlighten you regarding the development of employees. Teachers are employed by institutions (typically referred to as Managerial Institute) whose sole aim is to create paranoia in future employees. When future employees start their academic pursuits in the First Grade, teachers are trained by the Managerial Institute to instruct all students that all of their activities are annotated in a "***permanent record.***" Throughout their academic studies, students are constantly "***warned***" by teachers that their actions are going in their "***permanent record.***" This creates a sense of paranoia within the students (later becoming employees) that someone is always watching them and that there is a written record of all of their activities (both good and bad).

When the student leaves academia and becomes an employee, they carry this perception of being watched on to the job.

As an employee makes the transition from academia to the job, their "***permanent record***" becomes their evaluation appraisals. As a manager, you can draw upon the employee's prior experiences with "***permanent records***" by subtly implying in day-to-day activities, "***That's going to be noted in your appraisal.***" This will cause the employee to flashback to all of those years in academia, where they were constantly in fear of having something going in their "***permanent record.***"

In preparing appraisals, it is important to remember that you're not the only one that will read an employee's appraisal. Upper management will read the appraisal, the employee will read the appraisal, and the employee may share the appraisal with others. For this reason, it is important to carefully word the appraisal. You must be subtle in your criticisms, you must appear to have concern for the employee, and you must have documentation to prove your statements. Employees are usually lazy and will typically only look at whether they passed or failed. They won't usually read the narrative. Consequently, you can "***Pass***" an employee, yet include statements in the narrative that paint the employee as a problem employee.

In addition, when you present the employee with their appraisal, you are in control. You begin by making casual comments about the weather, feigning interest in their personal life, and then, **SLAM**, you smack them with the question, "***How do you think you've done your job?***"

All of the bad things that the employee has thought of you will resurface. The employee will become agitated and anxious to have the meeting over. As you delay showing the employee their evaluation, the employee becomes more and more restless; eager for the meeting to be over. Just when the employee can't take any more, you show them their appraisal, and they will immediately sign the appraisal, just to get out of your presence, often without even noticing whether they passed.

***Lesson Learned***: Nothing says "***Power***" like "***Permanent Record.***"

## Is There a Doctor in the House?

An employee calls in sick and you know that they're goofing off. What do you do? It's simple, you call the employee at home. **STOP.**

Now pay attention. You don't just call them and bluntly ask whether they're goofing off or not. You call them and, with concern in your voice, explain that something has happened in the office and you need their help. It could be that you want to know where they put a work file, it could be that you need a telephone number, and it could be that you need details on a work product. It is important that you phrase your question, so as to make it clear that you're calling in reference to a work-related issue.

Another reason to contact an employee, when they're on sick leave, is to irritate them. They're on sick leave at home, trying to forget about work, and trying to relax. **BOOM**, you call and ask them a simple question (i.e., "Where did you the file on.....?") and then hang up. They will spend the rest of the day (using up their sick leave) thinking about the real reason why you called (i.e., Were you checking up on them? Do you know that they were goofing off? Etc.).

***Lesson Learned:*** A simple telephone call can make the sick sicker.

## Ammo Depot

Previously, you were advised that managing can be correlated with going to war. Now, think real hard, before you go into battle, what is something that you want behind you? No, no, no, not your mother. Something more tangible. Okay, you want to have a good supply of ammunition which is typically called an "***ammo depot***." In an ammo depot, you store your various bombs, ammunition, and other sundry types of explosives. Now, you're wondering, "***Can I really use explosives on employees***?" No, there are certain laws prohibiting the use of explosives against employees. However, you can use explosive devices in the form of written memoranda.

There is the old adage, "***A picture is worth a thousand words***." Unfortunately, unless you put your words down on paper, employees may have difficulty recalling your words and may even take liberties with the substance of your words (i.e., a little creative interpretation of what you said—the employees may even conspire to "***put words in your mouth***"). Subsequently, it becomes necessary to document your words in the form of memoranda (***NOTE: In addition, as most of your memorandums are trivial, a complete waste of paper, and you write so many memorandums, you can't be expected to remember the details of every single memorandum. For this reason, you should keep a file of your memoranda***).

In addition, you can use memoranda to chastise an employee. An example, you've told an employee that there is a specific way of performing a task, but the employee just doesn't follow your verbal directions. Now, you prepare a memorandum and distribute it to all employees outlining your verbal directions. When the employee still doesn't follow your directions (verbal and written), you can utilize a little sarcasm by asking (and dropping a little explosion), "***Didn't you get the memorandum***?" What can the employee say? They know that they received the memorandum and consequently will begin to stutter and become extremely agitated. You can outwardly act confused as to why the employee can't follow directions and show your utter disgust for the employee's failure through the employment of effective (if not grotesque) facial expressions. Inwardly you can laugh at the discomfort of the employee from being put on the spot (***NOTE: Before you antagonize an employee to the point where the employee wants to do you bodily harm, it's important to take certain precautions, such as making sure that your windows don't open, if you're in a high-rise building***).

You can never have too many memoranda. They become your ammo depot, where you can open your desk drawer, pull out a specific memorandum, and utilize it to chastise an employee. While you may be tempted to use real explosives, memoranda have a more lasting impact. Consider that once an explosion occurs, damage is incurred and then things go pretty much back to normal. However, when you drop a memoranda bomb, the employee not only suffers a concussion from the initial explosion, but then suffers secondary explosions by starting to think about all of the other memoranda you must have secreted in that desk drawer. These secondary explosions can occur at any time, and if you're lucky, when the employee is on his own time. Image, the employee is sitting at his house, enjoying a little liquid refreshment and watching the television, when, **BOOOOM**, they recall a memorandum about not drinking.

***Lesson Learned:*** Because memoranda can be explosive devices, never be caught without an appropriate memorandum.

## Circle the Wagons

Can one of your employees promote you? Not hardly, so there is really no reason to become one of the "***boys***" or seek their acceptance or become friendly with the employees. Employees are nothing and can only hinder your promotional opportunity. For this reason, you must do anything and everything to support your upper managers, even if it means giving up your own employees (they're not really "***your own employees***" any way, they're more like a piece of furniture, like a chair or desk).

An example. An employee does something wrong and comes to you for guidance. You play the role of a concerned supervisor (and even a friend) by telling the employee that it will be okay, but you do need a memorandum from the employee, just to document the incident. Once you get the memorandum, you call up your upper manager and tell them how bad the employee messed up, and after listening to their story and now reading their memorandum, you think that the employee is lying.

By acting concerned and listening to the employee, you ensure that the employee won't go around your back to upper management. By telling your manager about the incident and that the employee lied, you promote the image that you're on top of everything that's going on in the office.

You further cement your position as a manager by documenting to your managers that the involved employee is a trouble-maker and can't be trusted (this becomes invaluable in future incidents). By suggesting that the employee is lying, you further the concept that employees can't be trusted.

***Lesson Learned:*** Never miss an opportunity to sacrifice an employee to upper management.

## A Watched Employee Never Boils

There's an old adage, "***A watched kettle (or pot), never boils.***" This holds true with employees. If employees are under the belief that you're constantly watching them, then they won't boil, they'll just steam.

It's important to set up an office policy where employees are required to verbally tell you whenever they leave the office. This makes them come into your office, face you, and try to explain why they're leaving the office.

Here's a helpful tip. When you hear the footsteps of an employee approaching your office, pick up the telephone and pretend that you're talking to someone on the other end. When the employee enters your office, you can either express disgust that they're interrupting your telephone call or you can simply ignore them. Now, they have to wait until you're off the telephone to tell you why they're leaving the office. This can cause them to be late for appointments (this can also be used at appraisal time to show that the employee isn't punctual). It also causes them to function on your time schedule, not theirs'.

Never, never, let an employee get into the practice of leaving you written notes regarding their absence from the office. This makes it too easy on the employee and you will lose all control. If you give a direct order that an employee is to leave a note regarding their activities, it is important to insure that no one else in the office is aware of your directive. This can be cumbersome because the employee may start to wonder why no one else is required to leave notes or may start leaving the notes with other employees.

***Lesson Learned:*** Watching employees is similar to watching birds. Those that you want to study more closely, you shoot and have stuffed.

## Self-Fulfilling Prophecy

What makes a good employee? Nothing. Employees are by nature a trouble-causing, malcontent, surly, unintelligent, socially inept, and a mob-influenced rabble. They will use any means to usurp your authority, with their only goal being to run amuck.

How do you keep employees from running amuck? In educational theory, there is the concept of the "***Self-Fulfilling Prophecy.***" Basically, the theory suggests that you can form the mold of a child's development by telling the child (over and over) that they can't achieve a particular goal and that they're lacking intelligence. You can gear your interaction with the child based on this concept. The child will then become to believe (based on what you've told the child and your actions toward the child) that they can't achieve a particular goal and are unintelligent.

As employees are very similar to children, you can employ the same concept by telling employees that they're incompetent in performing their job duties and lack experience. When the employee makes a mistake (which is unavoidable), you reiterate that they are incompetent and inexperienced. After making a few mistakes (if no mistakes occur, make some up) and being told by you of their incompetence and inexperience, the employee will eventually accept that they are indeed incompetent and inexperienced. It is important to reach this goal with your employees, because once the employees believe themselves to be incompetent and inexperienced, then they will stop trying to usurp your authority and will recognize you for the absolute deity that you are. This is an important method in those rare occasions where an employee may have more experience than you.

***Lesson Learned:*** Like children, employees must be reminded of their weaknesses, over and over and over and over again.

## Do You Know What You're Doing?

As teachers are employed by the Managerial Institute, parents are also often utilized to train future employees. A common statement promoted by the Managerial Institute for parents to utilize in training their children is the following: ***"Do you know what you're doing?"*** While the parent is completely aware of the reasons why a child is doing something, they start the child thinking that maybe they don't really know what they're doing. This creates a sense of doubt in the child, who then begins to question why they're doing what they're doing.

The statement can be used in any situation. As an example, the child is getting ready to drink some milk and the parent asks, "***Do you know what you're doing***?" The child then thinks, "***Maybe I shouldn't be drinking milk***" or "***Maybe there's something wrong with the milk***" or "***Should I have waited to get permission to drink the milk?"*** Basically, what was a simple act, now, becomes an intellectual challenge.

Knowing that the statement, "***Do you know what you're doing***" has been used in making a child feel guilty, the effective manager will employee the same statement in the job environment.

As an example, when an employee makes a request for vacation, first ascertain the employee's current leave balance and then ask, "***Do you know what you're doing***?" This does two (2) things:

1. It makes the employee stop and think whether they really should take vacation; and

2. It makes the employee believe that you don't think that they should be taking vacation.

***Lesson Learned:*** Only you know what's good for an employee.

## Hide And Seek

As a child, did you ever play the game, "***Hide and Seek***?" If not, the game involves one person covering their eyes, while others hide. The first person then attempts (seeks) to find the other people who hid. The winner is the one that isn't found. What ***does "Hide and Seek*"** have to do with managing employees? Quite simply, what an employee doesn't know (hidden) makes you a winner.

One utilization of the "***Hide and Seek***" approach is through the creation of "***Drop Files.***" What is a "***Drop File***"? A "***Drop File***" is a file that you keep on each employee that really isn't an official file and subsequently isn't available for review by the employee. This can be likened to a treasure chest. You place valuable and priceless tidbits of information concerning the employee into a file. These tidbits can be such things as notes that the employee was insubordinate to you, the employee was late for work, the employee doesn't get along with other employees, and any other thing that will help you to paint the employee as incompetent and a trouble-maker. In the event of any internal investigations on you, you simply open up the treasure chest and pull out a jewel of sentiment about the employee.

In the event that you transfer and a new manager arrives on site, you can use these "***Drop Files***" to acquaint the new manager with the problem employees and predispose the new manager to treating the employees appropriately.

***Lesson Learned:*** What an employee doesn't know will assist in their demise.

## Are You Blaming Me?

A story was once circulated involving an incident that reportedly occurred in a law enforcement agency. As the story goes, there was an occasion where a search warrant was executed (a search warrant being that event where police officers enter a person's home, in order to obtain specific evidence of the crime that the subject was alleged to have committed—a search warrant spells out what can be searched and what can be retained as evidence). As a general rule, the execution of search warrants are usually a dirty and sweaty business, as the officers conducting the search warrant are required to go through an entire residence, to include the attic, garage, and other often dirty places. Subsequently, the officers usually wear casual attire and are almost always armed, in the event that a subject becomes hostile.

During the execution of this particular search warrant, the supervisor arrived on the scene wearing a coat and tie (and leaving his firearm in the office). The supervisor then noticed that some firearms were discovered and immediately directed that the firearms be seized and retained (***NOTE: Firearms were not included in the search warrant as either evidence of the crime or something to be searched***). The officers on site attempted to explain that the firearms couldn't be seized, but the supervisor demanded that the firearms be seized on the basis that the subject might use the firearms to commit suicide. The officers then questioned the supervisor, "***If the subject represents the potential of committing suicide, then shouldn't the subject be placed in protective custody***?" The supervisor laughed this away and said, "***No, just seize the guns and let's get out of here***" (before the search was completed).

After the search warrant was completed and the officers left the scene, the subject found a piece of rope and started to swing from the ceiling (without the use of his hands and with the rope wrapped around his neck). When word of the suicide reached the office, an office meeting was convened. When the supervisor was apprised that the subject committed suicide, he became extremely agitated and demanded, "***Are you blaming me***?"

***Lesson Learned:*** When an employee makes an accusation, ask a question. This diverts attention from you and raises the issue of whether the employee is capable of knowing anything.

## That's Not What I Meant

Another story involving a law enforcement agency detailed a manager's manipulation of words. As the story goes, a manager would often direct his subordinates to engage in specific types of activities. This manager's directions would be very strict and would go from point to point, often with diagrams being drawn for the slower employees.

An example. The manager once told an employee to conduct surveillance on a suspect. Per directions from the supervisor, the surveillance would entail that the employee follow the suspect one block at a time (as in city block), until the surveillance showed the suspect meeting with other suspects.

After following the supervisor's directions, the employee subsequently detailed that the surveillance had been blown (discovered) because the suspect became suspicious of the same car following him, one block a day, for several days. The employee, in an act of pure insubordination, advised the manager that the surveillance was blown because of the manager's directions (one block a day).

The manager, in classic managerial finesse, made the statement, "***That's not what I meant.***" What could the employee say? Absolutely nothing, as it was the employee's fault for not fully understanding what the supervisor meant. In addition, as the employee was below the supervisor on an intellectual level, how could the employee possibly argue the meaning of the supervisor's initial directions? The supervisor found in this one incident a statement that could be used over and over again. Whenever employees would follow the manager's directions and something would go wrong, the manager would use the same statement, "***That's not what I meant.***"

***Lesson Learned:*** You say tomato, I say tomato'. While you are an attractive manager, you weren't selected for a managerial position because of your "***good looks.***" You were selected because you are indeed superior to employees. What can a lowly employee really know what it is that you meant?

## Su Casa es Mi Casa (Your House is My House)

People enjoy mysteries because of the suspense; they don't know how the story will end. There was a manager, who being extremely upset that someone had been given the access code to the back-door of the office, decided that he needed to approach the issue in a novel manner (***NOTE: The person that was given access had been assisting the office on significant projects***). The manager gave this matter a lot of thought and even reportedly consulted with his wife, in order to find the perfect words. The manager decided that the best way to approach the issue was to conduct an office meeting with his employees.

The manager set the initial tone of the meeting by issuing a written notice that there would be a mandatory meeting on such-and-such day. When the meeting started, the manager showed no sign of agitation, but rather started the meeting with general administrative business (kinda easing up on the subject). Then the manager made the statement that he needed house keys from all of the employees by the end of the day.

You can imagine the reaction. Employees started sweating and raised the question as to why the manager wanted keys to their houses. Some employees wondered whether the manager had the legal right to make such a request. In unison, the employees were confused.

The manager then artfully related that he had discovered that someone in the office had given access to the backdoor to another person. The manager then related that the employees' response to giving him (the manager) access to their houses was the same response he experienced when he discovered that someone had been given access to the backdoor of the office. What followed was an example of a complete disregard for authority. The employees all expressed the sentiment that they would have no problem giving the keys to their houses to the person that was given to the backdoor because they trusted him. However, they had a huge problem with giving keys to their houses to the manager because they didn't trust him.

***Lesson Learned:*** If you can't dazzle them with brilliance, then confuse them with the absurd. Remember, as a supervisor, you write the script and you set the stage for any theatrics in your office.

## Shooting Stars

There was a business wherein an employee filed several Equal Employment Opportunity (EEO) complaints and reported misconduct, abuses of authority, waste and fraud, allegations against a particular supervisor. Despite reporting numerous serious allegations, the employee continued to perform their job duties in a superior fashion and won praise from other managers. In many circles, the employee was considered on his way to the top; a rising star.

However, sensing that the employee was a viable threat, the manager (the subject of the allegations) devised a plan whereby he was able to effectively discredit the subordinate. The simplicity of the plan was pure genius. In essence, the supervisor wouldn't allow the employee to perform their duties. This was accomplished by disapproving the employee's requests for resources, with these resources being highly instrumental in the employee's completion of their job duties. The supervisor further insured that any special projects that looked promising (i.e., would make the employee look good) were assigned to other employees. The supervisor further began a systematic process of disapproving all of the employee's written reports, making the employee re-write and re-write and re-write reports for minor and non-existent errors. When the employee expressed their frustration about not being allowed to complete their job duties, due to the supervisor, the supervisor conducted a one-on-one session with the employee.

During this closed-door meeting (no other witnesses), the supervisor related that the employee was a trouble-maker for having filed EEO complaints and having made allegations against him (the supervisor). The supervisor then stated that he would do anything to get rid of the employee and would not allow the employee to complete any work projects. The supervisor stated, in the event he was interviewed by EEO or other investigating units, that he would use this inability of the employee to complete work projects as evidence that the employee was incompetent and inexperienced.

The manager then questioned the employee how he was going to prove that he was indeed competent and experienced, if he couldn't complete work projects.

Finally, the manager reiterated that he would do anything, to include making false statements and creating false memoranda, to get rid of the employee. The supervisor carried through with his threats and in all EEO investigations and other inquiries, he made claims that the employee was incompetent and inexperienced, and used the employee's failure to complete work projects as evidence. And, as expected, the supervisor denied ever having the closed door meeting with the employee.

***Lesson Learned:*** Whatever you say to an employee, in a one-to-one session, can never be used against you, because it becomes your word against the employee. Also, as highlighted above, the supervisor was successful in not only carrying through on his threats, but also letting the employee know who was really in charge of the employee's "***career***."

## Measuring the Immeasurable

There is often the belief among managers that you can only be as good as your employees. This is untrue.

A small outpost office of a major business was responsible for producing statistics which far exceeded the statistics of much larger offices. This outpost also was responsible for initiating work projects that had become recognized on a national basis for being highly significant. The employees assigned to this small outpost worked long hours, while the manager would often take extended lunch breaks, leave work early, and generally took no interest or active participation in the work projects being conducted by his employees. The day of appraisals, the manager rated all of his employees the same, barely successful. When given the opportunity to reward his employees, the manager replied that they hadn't'done anything special.

However, when this manger received his appraisal rating, he won glowing acclaim, with the work projects completed by his employees being the crowing glory. The manager was congratulated on his direction of the work projects and his expertise in resolving problems. The manager was commended on making not only the small outpost shine as a highly productive office, but also that through his efforts (the statistics of the outpost) that the whole organization shined. The manager was not only awarded an "***Excellent***" evaluation rating, but also received a significant monetary award.

***Lesson Learned:*** Take credit where credit can be found.

## Work For Yourself

There was a supervisor, who had the misfortunate of supervising an employee, who believed that they (the employee) had more experience and expertise in the job, than the supervisor. This employee would constantly question the supervisor regarding why they (the supervisor) wanted something done a certain way. This employee would constantly question the legality of what the supervisor wanted done. This employee would constantly bring up the issue that the supervisor's directions were against company policy and procedure. This employee would constantly bring up that the rights of other employees were being violated. In essence, this employee was a trouble-maker, who hadn't come to realize that the supervisor was an all-knowing person, who had absolute authority (rights and laws are to be applied at the discretion of a supervisor).

When the supervisor finally reached his limit of dealing with this employee's constant questioning of his (the supervisor) directions, the supervisor sent the employee an email message stating, "***If you can't handle being supervised, maybe you should work for yourself.***" In order to drive this point home, the supervisor attached the email message to the disapproval of a report prepared by the employee. In addition, in order to create a little bit of stress and disrupt the employee's weekend (time away from work), the supervisor sent the email on a Friday afternoon.

***Lesson Learned:*** If an employee doesn't want to accept your authority, then show them the door (***Note: It doesn't matter whether you have the authority or not***).

## Road Trip

In an office, located in close proximity to the Mexico-United States border, there was a frequent occasion for managers and an occasional subordinate (primarily selected to do the driving and finding cultural sites of interests) to travel into Mexico, in the company vehicle, for the purposes of cultural immersion, with this immersion occurring in, let's see, what would be a politically correct term? Brothel? House of Ill Repute? Whatever the politically correct term, these managers would pay for the company of ladies. The managers would also indulge in the tasting of tequila, with this tasting requiring substantial amounts of tequila. The managers and the selected subordinates would then travel, again in the company vehicle, back into the United States.

When one of the managers flew up the career ladder and his former subordinate jokingly referenced their trips to Mexico, the manager became incoherent and suffered an immediate memory lapse where he couldn't remember any of the details. After the encounter, the manager then found some reason to have the subordinate transferred to a significantly less pleasurable assignment.

***Lesson Learned:*** Remember, that was then and this is now. A secondary lesson would be that distance makes a witness either grow fonder or dampens his voice.

## Say "Cheese"

A story was once circulated involving an incident that reportedly occurred in a law enforcement agency. As the story goes, there was an occasion where a supervisor became intimately involved in an ongoing investigation. When several of his employees expressed their concern that the supervisor had not contacted other law enforcement agencies, in order to ascertain parallel investigations, the supervisor became indignant. The manager knew more than his employees and his agency was the only agency that mattered.

Well, on one occasion, the manager decided to become personally involved in the investigation by conducting surveillance of a particular business. Again, the supervisor ignored the pleas of his employees to check with other law enforcement agencies and proceeded to the business location. Of course, the supervisor was dressed in his normal attire, which included a brightly colored tie and a suit coat. The supervisor pulled his vehicle up to the front of the business and marched up to the front window. Being extremely covert, the manager then approached the nearest window, placed his hands up to the window, and peered in. Well, to his surprise, he immediately was confronted with a bright flash and couldn't see into the building. The manager concluded that the business was no longer operating and departed the scene.

Shortly after the manager completed his covert surveillance of the above business, one of his employees received an urgent telephone call from another law enforcement agency. This other agency was hysterical; something had just happened on one of their investigations. Some guy, dressed in a brightly colored tie and wearing a suit coat, had arrived at an undercover business location and had peered into their camera, just as the camera went off. The other law enforcement agency made some mention about using the resulting photograph for a recruitment poster for managers.

***Lesson Learned:*** If you're going to get involved in something where there's a slight chance you may be wrong, then use a disguise.

## Job Descriptions

As is often the case with managers, there was a manager who felt the necessity of working late in his office. Of course, what is a manager without someone to manage? So, the manager would have an employee also work late with him. On one particular occasion, the manager and the employee were locked in what could be loosely defined as an intense and intimate encounter, when a member of the cleaning staff walked in on them. Evidently the cleaning person had never been through a biology class wherein the topic of reproduction was discussed, because the cleaning person shrieked and went running down the halls.

***Lesson Learned:*** There's a lock on your office door for a reason.

## Foreign Affairs

On one occasion, an upper manager for a prestigious company had the opportunity to visit a foreign country, in order to learn their customs. During his stay, the manager had the occasion to encounter a young female who was exercising by walking up and down a particular street. Being ignorant of the exchange rate of the foreign country and desiring to broaden his knowledge of the local customs, the manager questioned the young lady about the cost of sexual favors. To his astonishment, the young lady was an uncover police officer, who subsequently arrested the manager for solicitation. Of course, in order to avoid an international incident, the matter was quickly and quietly resolved.

***Lesson Learned:*** Always ask the taxi driver about local customs.

## Dance Partners

Ever feel like hitting an employee? Ever feel like strangling an employee?

On one occasion, a manager took exception to an employee's job performance and started to strangle them. A second employee walked in and caught the incident. The manager was subsequently arrested and was allowed to spend the night in the local jail considering the errors of her mistake. The employee became a hero to the other employees for having caused the arrest of the manager.

***Lesson Learned:*** When caught with your hands around the throat of an employee, use the explanation that it's a new style of dance.

## Bulimia

The distance from the earth to the sun can be used as an example of how far you are removed from scrutiny. You're a manager. Your appraisal is done by a manager. Your promotions are decided by a manager. Your allegations are acted upon by a manager. Any disciplinary action taken against you is done by a manager. Are you getting the point? In this world, it's the managers against the employees. As a manager, you can always count on another manager taking your side over an employee.

There was a manager, who had the misfortunate of offending another manager, with this other manager taking disciplinary action against the first manager. This disciplinary action became part of the manager's personnel file. The manager learned his lesson and proceeded to win back the favor of the other manager, as well as every other manager. As time went on, a decree went forth which declared that anyone being considered for a promotion had to go through a "***vetting***" process. This "***vetting***" process involved a review of the prospective employee's personnel file. In the event that prior disciplinary action was disclosed, then the employee would not be promoted.

Oh me, oh my, what's a person to do? More aptly stated, "***What's a manager to do***"? A decree is a piece of paper. A disciplinary action is a piece of paper. The manager called in some favors and the disciplinary action mysteriously found its way into a shredder. The manager was awarded his promotion and his loyalty to the managers who operated the shredder (***WRITER'S NOTES: In an era of computer files, it is important to also purge (shred) all computer files relating to any offense—leave no trace***).

***Lesson Learned:*** A shredder isn't used just for making confetti for your parties.

## It's Not Written in Stone

There is the old adage that the only certain things are taxes and death. The majority of employees like to believe that they have control over certain things in their job. This is why employees like to work a straight shift, like from 9:00 to 5:00. They like to know that they have to be at work at 9:00 and that they can leave at 5:00. In the area of evaluation appraisals, employees like to believe that they are being evaluated by a certain set of guidelines. For example, they like to know that they have to produce 100 widgets, in order to receive a passing evaluation. Now, think for a minute. How can you utilize the employee's need for order? It's simple, you disrupt the order.

There was a manager who had a problem employee, in the sense that the employee was constantly filing complaints. Despite these complaints, the employee always exceeded his job requirements and constantly won praise from other companies for his outstanding work. The manager desperately wanted to either get rid of this employee and/or severely tarnish the employee's character. The manager thought and thought about how he could accomplish his goals. The manager then realized that an evaluation appraisal stayed with an employee **FOREVER**. The manager then started looking at the evaluation criteria for the employee trying to identify an area where the employee wasn't performing. The manager couldn't find a single weakness. In a moment of pure inspiration, the manager thought, "***Why don't I just make up a new criteria element***?"

The manager noted that the employee wasn't skilled in another language and swiftly penned the following appraisal criteria, "***Ability to Speak a Foreign Language***", into the employee's appraisal. Of course, since the employee didn't speak a foreign language, he received a lower evaluation appraisal rating. Of course the employee complained, but the company backed the manager and the appraisal remained. On the basis of this lower evaluation appraisal rating, the employee was precluded from promotions.

***Lesson Learned:*** While employees may mistakenly believe that some things are written in stone, the only certainty is the authority of a supervisor.

## Please Mr. Postman

In a particular office, there was a manager who sent forth a decree that all mail coming into the office was official mail and subsequently he had the authority to open all mail. You have to follow a decree don't you? So, the manager would often take his lunch break at his desk and open the incoming mail which often included personal mail for his employees. This activity not only provided the manager with some laughs, but also some ammunition for future encounters with his employees.

What's a decree? As fate would have it, on one occasion, the manager received personal mail and, according to the decree, was opened by the secretary. After this incident, the decree became refined to state that all mail coming to the office for **EMPLOYEES** was official and subsequently could be opened. However, as he was the manager (the top person), no one else could open mail addressed to the manager.

***Lesson Learned:*** Decrees are ruled by the degree of the direct involvement of a manager. As a manager, the rules only apply to you, if you so desire.

## I Didn't Order That

There was a manager who assumed control of a particular office. To his astonishment, the employees seemed to like his predecessor more than him. In an act of anticipation of future supply problems, this manager's predecessor had ordered a large amount of copier paper which was stored in the office.

The new manager decided that there was no need for all of this copier paper (besides the other boss had ordered it), so he ordered it destroyed. After destroying reams and reams of paper and then waiting an appropriate amount of time (rumor has it that this "***appropriate amount of time***" was only a few minutes), the manager had new paper ordered.

***Lesson Learned:*** It's not being wasteful, if you make the decision.

## Check Your Personal Life at the Door

From the day that a manager is born, they are trained to assume their ultimate goal of becoming a manager. Their lives become structured to ensure that all of their activities are focused on becoming a manager. This may include marrying the "***right***" person, attending the "***right***" college, buying a house in the "***right***" neighborhood, and belonging to the "***right***" clubs. When a manager becomes a manager, they continue this trend by devoting their entire life (both on the job and away from the job) to management. In realizing how happy they are being a manager and devoting their lives to managing employees, managers predictably believe that employees should share the same attitude that the job is everything.

However, employees often complain about working long hours, working on weekend, having to travel on short notice, and having to cancel personal plans. This is what makes a manager's job difficult; employees wanting to have a personal life. Who knows best? Of course the manager knows what is best for the employee and, if it's deemed necessary, then the manager will issue the employee a personal life, designed to suit them best.

***Lesson Learned:*** If the company wanted you to have a personal life, then they would have issued you one.

## Comfort Vs Company Policy

There was an occasion where a manager discovered that his office furniture didn't suit his unique personality or physical structure (he was on the short side). Unfortunately, there was an existing company policy that prohibited the purchasing of new furniture, unless it was done through an existing contractor used by the company. The manager scoured this contractor's catalogue and could not find any furniture that even came close to meeting his specific needs and desires. How can you manage, if you're not comfortable?

Taking the initiative, the manager ordered furniture from another company that more closely matched his needs and desires. While this purchase did exceed prior expenditures for furniture, the manager was able to rationalize the expenditure by claiming that it was an emergency purchase. An emergency is an emergency and the manager was not only allowed to keep his new furniture, but was also commended on his ability to decisively react to an emergency.

***Lesson Learned:*** While company policies may exist, the unwritten policies governing managers reign supreme.

## Word Puzzles

Have you ever been a part of a conversation where the other person uses a word that you don't understand, but admitting that you don't know the word would be an admission that you're not as educated as the other person?

There was a manager who developed an extensive vocabulary and never missed an opportunity to display his command of the English language. One of this manager's favorite words was "***axiomatic***." The manager initially presented this word to his employees, during a rather intense discussion regarding the manager's grasp of a particular situation. When the manager's employees became somewhat hostile regarding why the manager had done something, he defensively responded, "***It's AXIOMATIC.***" Of course, the employees, having only progressed to the "***AS***" section in the dictionary, thought the manager was saying, "***It's ASININE.***"

The employees accepted the manager's defense that it was "***ASININE***" (stupid), rather than actually knowing that he was saying "***AXIOMATIC***" (self evident). The discussion ended, with both parties contented, but believing in different reasons for the peaceful conclusion: The manager believed that he had again astounded his employees with his wealth of knowledge and that they had accepted that the reason was self evident; and The employees came away believing that the manager had finally admitted his level of intelligence.

***Lesson Learned:*** It's not what you say, rather it's how you say it.

## Practice Makes Perfect

On one occasion, a manager was notified that a high ranking official would be visiting his city. The manager and his employees were given the opportunity to provide transportation for the official. Do you realize how difficult it is to meet someone at the airport and then transport them to their hotel?

Well, the manager realized the importance of conducting trial runs and made the appropriate preparations. The manager, acting as the visiting official (who else could play an official?), instructed his employees to meet him at the airport, act as though he was the visiting official, and then transport him to the hotel where the official would be staying. How many trial runs are necessary? The manager decided that it was necessary to have his employees pick him up at the airport and transport him to the selected hotel on several occasions.

In addition, it wasn't enough to just conduct the practice, the manager also had to time each practice session and the time that it took for each phase (i.e., parking the car, walking into the airport, meeting the official, getting his luggage, going to the car, opening the door, getting in the car, and then driving to the hotel). Of course these practice sessions took precedence over the work that was waiting at the office.

As a side-note, the visiting official arrived early on the appointed day and took a taxi to his hotel, leaving the manager waiting at the airport.

***Lesson Learned:*** Practice makes perfect.

## Personal Distractions

When employees are reminded of their personal lives, they tend to become distracted with their work. One manager recognized this tendency and noticed that employees would invariably decorate their cubicles with personal items, such as photographs of family members, postcards, calendars (not the ones issued by the company), little figurines, and other "stuff" that loudly voice the sentiment "I'M A REAL PERSON."

The manager consequently issued a directive that cubicles would cease to be cesspools of individual expressionism and that the personalizing of cubicles would immediately cease. The manager would then conduct periodic inspections (usually after the employees had left work for the day, allowing him the opportunity to peruse documents left inside employees' desks) of cubicles and annotate the presence of any personal objects that defied his directive.

The manager would then issue memoranda detailing violations of his directive. In addition, on those occasions when an employee seemed to be lost in thought at their desk, the manager would vehemently inform the employee that personal thoughts were a distraction to their completing their work assignments.

By removing the personal objects in the employees' cubicles, the manager was, in some small way, to aid in removing the potential of employees thinking about their lives. Face it, you see a picture of your mother, and you'll start thinking about your mother. If there's no picture, then it takes more concentration to think about your mother and, managers will agree that employees lack the ability to concentrate for extended periods of time.

***Lesson Learned:*** A distracted employee is an unproductive employee. And, an employee that is reminded of their life outside of the job, will be prompted to recall that they are a real person.

## Torture Tips

Since the first battle was waged and prisoners captured, torture has been an acceptable method of extracting information from individuals, whose first thought was not to provide information. Torture, effectively applied, allowed these individuals to forget this first thought and enthusiastically provide the requested information.

Torture has also been utilized in employer-employee relations, when employees have been reluctant to either obey commands or follow instructions. What employer hasn't wanted to break out the whip and stimulate a problem employee's motivation?

While physical torture (i.e., whips, placement on the rack, etc.) is perhaps the most recognizable form of torture, the application of mental torture is often overlooked as an effective tool in subduing unruly employees. This mental torture can include:

1. Telling an employee that they're useless.
2. Calling an employee derogatory names.
3. Making jokes about the employee (***NOTE: This is most effective when the jokes are told in front of other employees***).
4. Treating the employee as sub-human.

Due to the successful subversive plot by former supervisors, aided by disgruntled employees, the utilization of physical torture has become a "***no-no***" in managing employees.

No matter how much you would like to punch an employee, you cannot physically touch an employee. This only leaves you with the option of employing mental torture.

It should be noted that the effective utilization of mental torture can often result in physical side effects in the employee (i.e., sleepless nights, high blood pressure, ulcers, etc.).

***Lesson Learned:*** Through the use of mental torture, you can achieve both physical and mental disturbances, yet you're not liable for the physical torture. And, proving mental torture is extremely difficult.

# *Self Assessment*

Okay, you've been provided with direction on how to manage employees and you've been provided with classical examples of good management in practice. But, how do you know that you're a good manager? Answer the following questions:

| | Yes | No |
|---|---|---|
| Do your employees have derogatory nicknames for you? | | |
| Do your employees use a lot of sick leave and annual leave? | | |
| Do your employees wander the halls with a dazed look in their eyes? | | |
| Do your employees make comments about high blood pressure? | | |
| Are your employees constantly putting in for transfers? | | |
| Have your employees complained to upper management? | | |
| Have your employees filed any formal complaints? | | |
| Do your employees talk about you to other employees? | | |
| Do you hear or have you been told that employees call you an Idiot? | | |

If you answered "***Yes***" to all of the questions, you are indeed a successful manager.

However, if you answered "***No***" to any of the above questions, then you need more work in refining your management style.

# A Pointer After

As a manager, what have you learned?

There are countless examples of incidents wherein managers overcame the odds and reduced their employees to a shivering mass of unthinking robots. You can learn from these examples and you can pattern your managerial style after the classic managers of times past. However, all of this can be reduced to one motivating thought that will see you develop into a successful manager:

> ***An abused, victimized, and traumatized employee defines you as a good and successful manager.***

While the current book has been presented with the belief in the existence of "***idiot***" managers, the authors would like to take this opportunity to acknowledge that there are some really good managers out there. These managers are not only competent in performing their jobs, but also have a genuine concern for their employees. The authors express their thanks that, in their individual careers, they have worked for some really good managers and that the "***idiot***" manager has been a rarity.

While the appearance of an "***idiot***" manager may be seldom, the effects are often more lasting and detrimental to the employee, who subsequently experiences feelings of being abused, victimized, and traumatized.

# *About the Authors*

Dazed, Crazed, and Confused are employees of a multi-national company, who have found themselves periodically subjected to the managerial styles of an idiot.

# *Bibliography*

Hanzhang, General Tao, ***Sun Tzu's Art of War: The Modern Chinese Interpretation***, Sterling Publishing Company, Inc., 1987.

***Webster's New World Compact, Dictionary of American English***, Simon & Schuster, New York, 1981.

0-595-21283-2

Printed in the United States
29373LVS00006B/362

9 780595 212835